# Stocking Stuffers!

## CALM DOWN & COLOR!

'Just Calm the Fuck Down' and color with this brand new adult coloring book filled with flowery and mandala patterns. Includes regular coloring pages, midnight edition, and more!

## MAKE THEM LAUGH!

Make every adult you know laugh out loud when they see the 'Gag Gift of the Year!" This adult coloring book is jam-packed with coloring pages of animals gone wild from around the world!

**AVAILABLE ON AMAZON.COM!** (search title + John T)

Use this swear word adult coloring book during the holidays to help you relieve your stress and relax.

Especially, when dealing with family, in-laws, or neighbors that wreak havoc during the festivities.

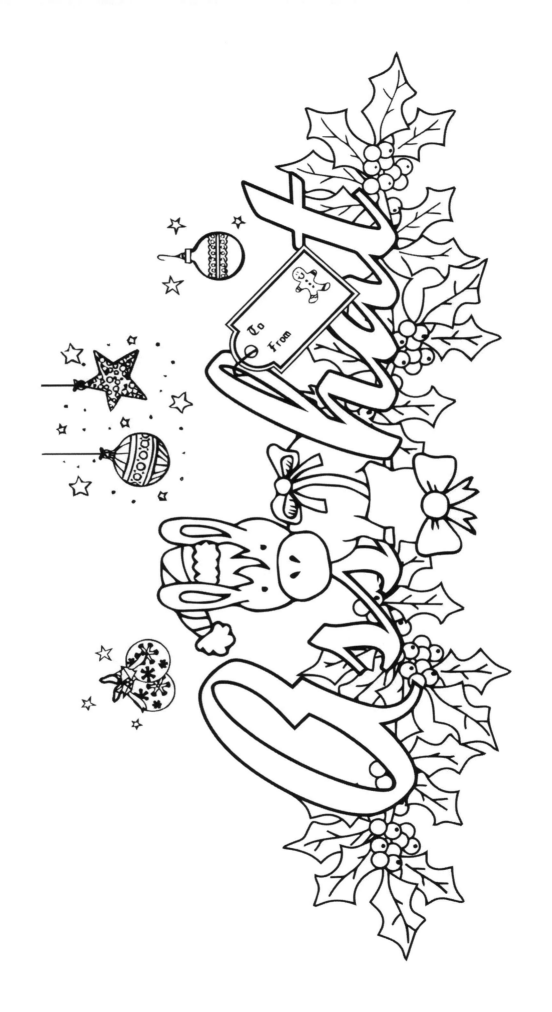

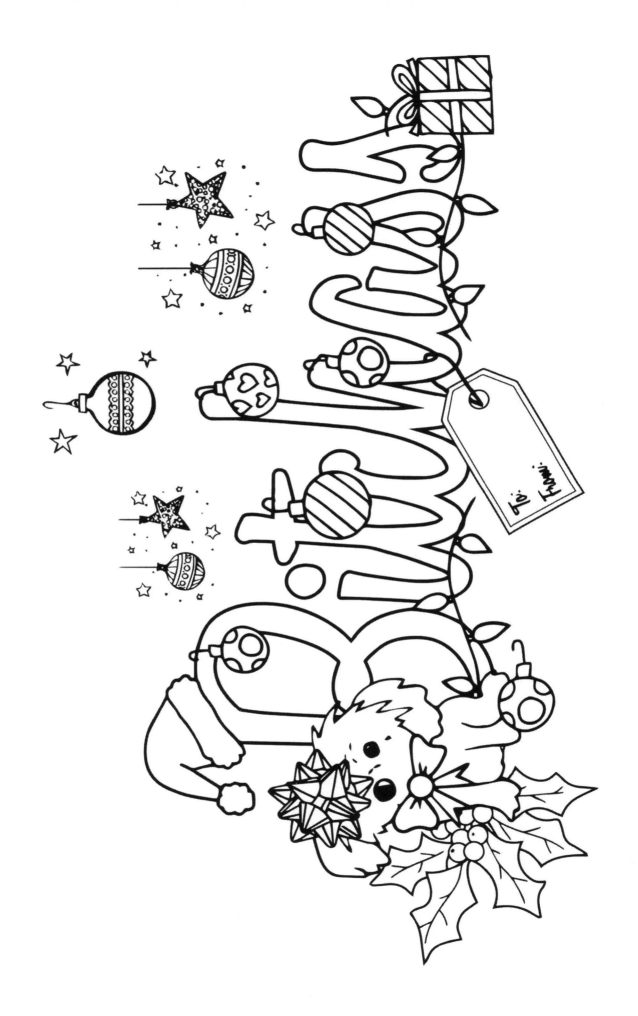

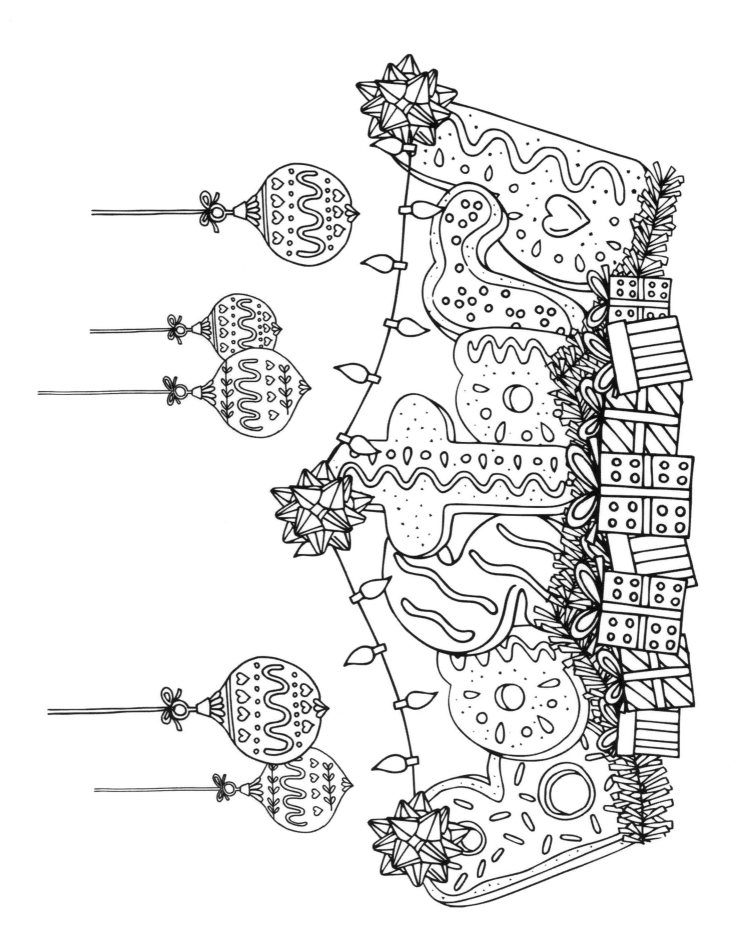

Made in the USA
Middletown, DE
17 December 2022

18737586R00027